T0198692

What is the BIBLE?

Written by
CHARLIE ROSE

Illustrated by
MARK BRAYER

WestBow Press books may be ordered through booksellers or by contacting:

WestBow Press
A Division of Thomas Nelson & Zondervan
1663 Liberty Drive
Bloomington, IN 47403
www.westbowpress.com
844-714-3454

Interior Image Credit: Mark Brayer

NLT:
• Scripture quotations marked (NLT) are taken from the Holy Bible, New Living Translation,
copyright ©1996, 2004, 2015 by Tyndale House Foundation. Used by permission of
Tyndale House Publishers, a Division of Tyndale House Ministries, Carol Strea..

ISBN: 978-1-6642-7167-8 (sc)
ISBN: 978-1-6642-7168-5 (e)

Library of Congress Control Number: 2022912498

Print information available on the last page.

WestBow Press rev. date: 07/23/2022

WESTBOW
P R E S S®
A DIVISION OF THOMAS NELSON
& ZONDERVAN

Dedication:

To my husband, Colby, thank you for your constant support. I feel blessed to be your wife and partner in advancing the gospel. This book would not have been possible without your love and encouragement.

To my daughter and son, Sophie and Samuel, I ask God daily to draw you both to Himself. Your lives have spurred me to write this book in hopes that it teaches you more about the Bible.

To my Lord and Savior, Jesus Christ, thank you for saving me. I pray this book brings glory to You.

Mommy and Daddy read the Bible every morning and every night.

Mommy and Daddy read the Bible every day, but I don't know why.

"Mommy, you love God. I know this is true.

I want to know God more, but it seems
hard to do...," said the child.

"You can know God," replied Mommy,
"He isn't far from you."

His purpose was for the nations
to seek after God and perhaps
feel their way toward him and
find him – though he is not far
from any one of us. (Acts 17:27)

Mommy loves the Bible, and
I think I should too.

I have a couple of questions and
want to know what to do.

When I read the Bible, I don't always understand.

Why is the Bible important? Is it really
written with God's hand?

Is the Bible all truth, or
could it have mistakes?

Is it better than other books,
or are they all just the same?

Daddy reads me the Bible, and I want to understand.

I think I'm going to ask him to help me. I know he can.

"The Bible is God's words given to man.

God gave us the Bible to know Him and His plan," explained Daddy.

All Scripture is inspired by God and useful to teach us what is true and to make us realize what is wrong in our lives. It corrects us when we are wrong and teaches us to do what is right. (2 Timothy 3:16)

"God sent His son Jesus to take away our sin, and now we can live with Him forever in a perfect place called Heaven!" Daddy exclaimed with joy!

For this is how God loved the world: He gave his one and only Son, so that everyone who believes in him will not perish but have eternal life. (John 3:16)

"Wow, what a win!" the child shouted.

"Since the Bible is from God, it always tells the truth.

No way could it ever lie; God would not allow it to."

Make them holy by Your truth; teach them Your word, which is truth. (John 17:17)

"The Bible is what we need to live a joyful life.

Yes, sad things still happen, but the Bible will help us get through all right," Daddy continued.

I have told you all this so that you may have peace in me. Here on earth, you will have many trials and sorrows. But take heart, because I have overcome the world! (John 16:33)

"The Bible teaches right from wrong and how to love our friends.

It's God's book to us, and we obey it simply because God says," Mommy said to the child.

If you love me, obey my commandments. (John 14:15)

"When you read the Bible and find it hard to understand, remember that God loves you and wants to help you know Him firsthand.

God has a purpose for you and me.

The Bible helps us tell others about Him so they can also see."

Therefore, go and make disciples of all the nations, baptizing them in the name of the Father and the Son and the Holy Spirit. Teach these new disciples to obey all the commands I have given you. And be sure of this: I am with you always, even to the end of the age. (Matthew 28:19-20)

"So, when you play outside and run fast with your friends,

or when it's raining, and you color until the markers come to an end,"

"When you take a bath and splash all around,
or when you're in time-out and
want to stomp and pout,"

"Remember, the
Bible is a book for
you and me.

The Bible is a book
we REALLY need
to read," Mommy
taught the child
and gave her a big
hug full of love.

Study this Book of instruction continually. Meditate on it day and night so you will be sure to obey everything written in it. Only then will you prosper and succeed in all you do. (Joshua 1:8)

Printed in the United States
by Baker & Taylor Publisher Services